How To St

Alcohol Today

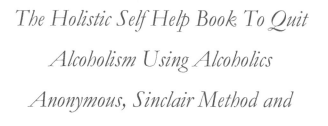

The Holistic Self Help Book To Quit

Alcoholism Using Alcoholics

Anonymous, Sinclair Method and

Naltrexone (Addiction Recovery Without

Too Much Willpower)

Martha B. Bailey

Bluesource And Friends

This book is brought to you by Bluesource And Friends, a happy book publishing company.

Our motto is **"Happiness Within Pages"**

We promise to deliver amazing value to readers with our books.

We also appreciate honest book reviews from our readers.

Connect with us on our Facebook page www.facebook.com/bluesourceandfriends and stay tuned to our latest book promotions and free giveaways.

Don't forget to claim your FREE books!

Brain Teasers:

https://tinyurl.com/karenbrainteasers

Harry Potter Trivia:

https://tinyurl.com/wizardworldtrivia

Sherlock Puzzle Book (Volume 2)

https://tinyurl.com/Sherlockpuzzlebook2

Also check out our best seller books

"67 Lateral Thinking Puzzles"

https://tinyurl.com/thinkingandriddles

"Rookstorm Online Saga"

https://tinyurl.com/rookstorm

Table of Contents

Introduction

Alcohol is one of the most used addictive, yet legal, substances in the US. In the US, one in 12 adults is dependent upon alcohol. Several million people drink heavily, but not all binge drinkers end up becoming alcoholics, although it is one of several factors in alcoholism.

Over the last year:

- 62.9% of women over 12 drank alcohol

- 68.6% of men over 12 drank alcohol

- 24.9% of drinkers said they binge drink

- 6.5% of drinkers said they drink heavily

- 5.9% met the criteria of a substance disorder

- 88,000 deaths each year are due to excessive alcohol use

How To Stop Drinking Alcohol Today

In the nation, alcoholism is the third leading cause of lifestyle-related death. In hospitals, around 40% of their beds are used to treat people who have health conditions related to alcohol use. Older people are hospitalized just as often for alcohol-related health issues as they are for heart attacks.

An overdose of alcohol is the cause of 2,200 deaths in the US every year, which is roughly six deaths daily. Some of the most common signs of alcohol overdose are:

- Low body temperature

- No gag reflex

- Clammy skin

- Slow heart rate

- Trouble breathing

- Seizures

- Vomiting

- Difficulty staying awake

- Confusion

Sometimes you can spot alcohol abuse easily. Then there are other times when it takes longer to show up. It is extremely important that you act quickly once the warning signs do appear. When you can catch alcoholism early on, it will improve your odds of making a healthy recovery.

Some of the most common signs of alcoholism are:

- Needing to drink more in order to get the same effects.

- A drop in performance and attendance at school or work.

- Doing everything you can to hide how much you drink.

- Placing alcohol at a higher importance than personal relationships and responsibilities.

How To Stop Drinking Alcohol Today

- Drinking despite its consequences.

- Spending less time doing things that you used to find important, like spending time with friends and family, pursuing hobbies, exercising, or doing other things you like.

- Unsuccessfully trying to limit how much you drink.

- Drinking even though you promised to quit.

- Not being able to control your drinking

- Experiencing withdrawal symptoms like fatigue, nausea, sweating, trembling, and shakiness.

Everybody has their own view as to what alcoholism looks like. A lot of people like to think alcoholics are akin to some homeless bag woman or man on the street. They appear disheveled and sick, with no purpose and no job.

How To Stop Drinking Alcohol Today

This isn't alcoholism, not always. In fact, the majority of alcoholics are high-functioning. They appear to have everything together on the outside. They make plenty of money, have nice cars, big houses, loving families, and a good job. But on the inside, they are ruled by alcohol.

Anybody can be an alcoholic. Very rarely does it fall into the stereotype that people have. Alcoholism doesn't play favorites nor differentiate based on the type of person it befalls. This means that there isn't a single person out there immune to this disease. The good news is, everybody can quit. All they need is some help.

Part One: The Holistic Approach

Is It A Disease Or A Habit?

The majority of people are rather confused by alcoholism and how it actually affects people. There are a lot of people out there who believe that it is just a lifestyle choice and that all a person has to do is stop. However, people who truly understand alcoholism, including treatment professionals and researchers who deal with this on a daily basis, know that there is a lot more to this.

In the US alone, the use of alcohol is legal for people over 21, is fairly easy to get and also inexpensive. The consumption of alcohol is socially accepted and is promoted. Most people are considered to be a light or moderate drinker, but there are some who engage in binge drinking.

How To Stop Drinking Alcohol Today

"Binge drinking" is defined by the National Institute on Alcohol Abuse and Alcoholism as drinking enough alcohol to raise your blood alcohol level to 0.08d/dL. This is normally about four drinks during a two hour period for women and five for men.

Alcoholism is a substance addiction, just like drugs. According to the American Society of Addiction Medicine, addictions are chronic diseases that affect the motivation, reward, and memory parts of the human brain. This will then lead to dysfunctions in a person's spiritual, social, emotional, mental, and physical life. Like with all other chronic illnesses, there isn't a cure for alcoholism, but there are treatments that can help a person to manage their condition.

Alcoholism refers to a disorder where a person is not able to control their alcohol use, continues using it even once it causes problems, or is preoccupied with alcohol. This will create unsafe levels of alcohol consumption. Most of the time, they will consume large quantities of alcohol in just two hours.

There are several alcohol-use disorders, alcoholism being the most severe. With any alcohol-use disorder, there should still be a concern as they can eventually end up causing alcoholism if they aren't handled.

A Disease

At the turn of the century, between the 19th and 20th, addicts were viewed as morally wrong and they were even shunned as sinners or bad people. These viewpoints are what led the physicians of the time to change how people viewed alcoholics in order to help them instead of punishing them.

By the 1930s, when Alcoholics Anonymous was formed and E. M. Jellinek published his book that defined the concept of alcoholism, alcoholism was pushed into a different view. Jellinek is the father of the disease theory of alcoholism. He listed alcoholism in different stages that drinkers will work through.

How To Stop Drinking Alcohol Today

The stages include:

1. Pre-alcoholic – This includes social drinking and is where drinkers will start to build up a tolerance for alcohol and start drinking in order to feel better or relieve stress.

2. Prodromal phase – This is the early stage of alcoholism and is where blackouts normal occur. The drinker will often start drinking alone and secretly, and they often think about alcohol as their tolerance to the substance begins to grow.

3. Crucial phase – This is characterized by an out-of-control spiral of drinking. They drink at inappropriate times and problems with their regular life start to occur, as well as physical changes in the body and brain.

4. Chronic phase –This includes daily drinking. Drinking has become the main focus of a person's life. They experience more health

problems, withdrawal symptoms and cravings and long-term mental and physical abuse problems.

Alcohol depresses the central nervous system and because its molecules are small in size, it is able to affect several parts of the body and brain at the same time. Alcohol messes with the chemistry of the brain. It starts out by increasing neurotransmitters that affect the pleasure centers of the brain, but with chronic use, it depletes them. As a person's tolerance increases, the user has to drink more to feel the same effects, which hurts them even more.

Alcoholism is likened to a medical illness by the NCADD through the disease model. This disease model depends on there being a physical addiction that can't be controlled, and is distinguished by certain symptoms and requires medical treatment. Periods of cravings and withdrawal symptoms are all part of the reason why alcoholism is considered a disease.

This model doesn't necessarily take into account why people become addicted while others don't. To figure out the reason why, you have to look at environmental and cultural factors, as well as traumatic events. Growing from this model, professionals started looking at addiction as being hereditary or genetic. This theory explains that addicts might have predispositions towards addiction, or genes that could help to figure out if a person ends up becoming an alcoholic.

A lot of people believe that a combination of environmental factors and genes lead to addiction. Others argue that addiction is simply a psychological symptom and not an actual disease.

Chronic Disease

I've mentioned that alcoholism is categorized as a chronic disease. Before we look at this further, let's define exactly what a chronic disease is:

How To Stop Drinking Alcohol Today

A chronic disease is a disease that lasts more than three months. It cannot be prevented by a vaccine, it can't be cured through medicine, and it won't simply go away. Chronic diseases typically impact older adults, with about 88% over people over 65 having at least one chronic disease.

Some other types of chronic diseases are oral issues, obesity, colon and breast cancer, cardiovascular disease, and arthritis. Chronic disease is the main cause of death and disability in the US. Seven out of ten deaths every year is due to a chronic disease. Most chronic disease can be treated or managed through medications and lifestyle changes.

Chronic diseases will continue to get worse when treatment is avoided. This is an important part of the definition to remember when it comes to alcoholism.

So, alcoholism as a chronic disease means that it requires ongoing and indefinite treatment in order to control the symptoms. Another aspect of it being a chronic illness is that there is a risk of relapse. When it comes to alcoholism and other addictions, the rate of relapse is close to those of others with chronic psychological and physical disorders. For instance, the rate of relapse for people with diabetes or asthma is 30 to 50 percent and 50 to 70 percent, respectively. The rates of relapse for addictions are 40 to 60 percent.

This means that alcoholism is a disease and not a habit. But, it can be argued that the disease may be started by a bad habit that grew into something that couldn't be controlled.

Take The First Step And Set A Goal

The first thing you need to do once you realize you have a problem is to set your first goal. In order to succeed at giving up drinking, you have to set goals. Without a goal, you won't have any direction and focus. Goal setting will give you the ability to take control of the direction of your life, as well as providing you with a benchmark to figure out if you are succeeding.

Look at it this way – If you had a million dollars in your bank account, it would only be proof that you have succeeded in your goal to amass a fortune. If, instead, your goal was to give to charity, keeping all of that money for yourself goes against your definition of success.

In order to set and accomplish goals, you need to know the best way to set them. Saying "I want to stop drinking," is a great first step, but it isn't enough to make the change. Goal setting is a process. You have to start with careful consideration of the things that you would like to achieve, and then end it through hard work in order to achieve it. Between these two things are some important steps that go beyond the actual goal. When you know these steps, you will be able to come up with goals that you are able to accomplish.

The Golden Rules Of Goal Setting

The following are the five most important rules that you need to follow to set a goal that you will stick to:

1. The goal should motivate you.

When you are setting a goal, you have to make sure that it motivates you. This means that they should be important to you in some way, and that you find value in achieving your goal. If you aren't that interested in the outcome of the goal, or they aren't important in the bigger picture, then you likely won't put all the work that you need to in order to achieve them.

How To Stop Drinking Alcohol Today

Motivation is one of the most important parts of achieving a goal.

You need to create goals that relate to the big priorities in your life. If you don't focus on the most important things, you may well end up with way too many goals, and you won't have enough time to achieve them. In order to achieve goals, you have to commit to your goals. In order to increase your chance of success, you need to have some sense of urgency. If this isn't present, then there is a risk of putting off the things you need to do in order to reach your goal. This will cause you to feel frustrated and disappointed in yourself, which will only de-motivate you. This can put you in a destructive place, and when it comes to alcoholism, this isn't a place you want to be.

2. Be SMART with your goals.

You've likely already heard about SMART goals, but do you know how to make them? The only way a goal can be powerful is if they are SMART. There are a few definitions of SMART, but essentially your goal needs to be:

- Specific

- Measurable

- Attainable

- Relevant

- Time-Bound

Your goal needs to be well defined and clear. A vague goal isn't going to be very helpful because they won't help guide you. You want to make sure that your goals can show you the way. You want to make your goals as easy as possible to be able to get wherever it is that you want to go by defining exactly where you want to end up.

You want to include precise dates, amounts, and anything else that can help you to measure your success. You can't simply say that your goal is to quit drinking. How are you going to know that you have been successful? How long do you plan on taking you to stop drinking? Without a way to measure success, you are going to miss out on celebrating your achievements.

You also need to make sure that your goal is attainable. If you have created a goal that is in no way attainable, you are only going to erode your confidence. However, you shouldn't set goals that are way too easy. Reaching a goal that wasn't that hard to achieve is going to feel anticlimactic, and can make you feel afraid of setting more goals in future as you may feel like you didn't do anything. By creating goals that are attainable and challenging, you will reach the balance you need. These will make you push out of your comfort zone and will give you the most satisfaction.

Your goals also need to be relevant to how you would like your life to continue. By making sure your goals stay in line with your life, you will have the focus you need in order to get ahead in life. If you set goals that are inconsistent and scattered, you are going to fritter your time away.

Your goals have to have a deadline. This gives you a chance to celebrate the success you achieve. When you have a deadline, you will have a greater sense of urgency and you will achieve more.

3.   Put your goals in writing.

Physically writing down your goals will make them more tangible and real. You won't have any excuse for forgetting about your goals. When you write your goals down, make sure that you use the word "will" and not words like "might" or "would like to." Using weak words won't give your statement as much power as it needs to make sure that you achieve your goals.

It may also help to post your goals in a visible place to help remind you each and every day of what it is that you want to achieve. Places like your bathroom mirror, computer, refrigerator, desk, or wall are perfect.

4. Create an action plan.

This is normally a missed step in the goal-setting process, and that's making an action plan. People become so focused on the outcome that they tend to forget to make a plan of the steps that they need to make to reach it. By coming up with the steps, and then marking them off when you achieve them, you will be able to see that you are making progress towards your goal. This is a very important step when your goal is demanding, big, or long-term.

5. Make sure you stick with it.

Quitting drinking is an ongoing process. Create reminders in order to keep yourself on track. It also helps to set aside time every day, week, or month to review how you are going. Your end goal is likely going to remain the same, but the steps it takes to get to them is probably going to change. You have to make sure that you keep your necessity, value, and relevance high.

Now that we know the best way to make a goal, let's walk through an example of how to set a goal to give up alcohol.

Action Plan

1. Write down an area in your life where you would like to see improvements. This is likely going to be giving up alcohol.

2. Create your SMART goal to achieve this. In order to give up alcohol safely, you may want to try step-down goals to slowly reduce your consumption. This can lessen the intensity of withdrawal symptoms. The only thing about this method is that you need to enlist the help of somebody who will monitor you to make sure that you actually stick to your plan of tapering off. For this, your SMART goal could look like this:

How To Stop Drinking Alcohol Today

a. Specific – I am going to slowly reduce my intake of alcohol by one drink every day until I no longer have a drink a day.

b. Measurable – I will write it in my journal every day until I reach my goal of reducing my alcohol intake.

c. Action-oriented/Attainable – I will make sure I have plenty of teas and sparkling water to drink, and during the time that I can still drink, I will only do so after eating. I will also read an article every day about alcohol abuse.

d. Reasonable/Relevant – I will let my support team know what I am planning on doing and I will ask them for help whenever I need support.

e. Time-based – I will check in with a
    support member every single week.
    After a month has passed, I will check
    in to see how well I have done in
    giving up alcohol.

This is just one example of what your goal can look
like. The important thing is to make sure you do
anything and everything you can to make sure you
reach your goal.

Out Of Sight, Out Of Mind

The next step on the road of recovery is to get rid of all the alcohol in your house. This is probably the easiest thing to do, but in your mind, it's going to be very hard. You have been dependent on alcohol for a long time, and it's going to feel like you are throwing out a friend.

If you need to, you can ask somebody you trust to help you get rid of the alcohol. How you dispose of the alcohol will depend on where you live. If you have your own septic system, you should be able to dispose of two bottles without messing with your septic system. You may want to wait a couple of weeks before you pour any more down the drain. If you are on a public sewer system, you can pour all of it down the drain because the treatment facility will keep the wastewater treated.

You don't want to overlook this step. The more you see something in your house, the more you are going to want it. This is no different than a person getting rid of junk food in their home when they want to lose weight.

Now that all of the temptations are out of your house, you need to take a look at the people you surround yourself with. There is no way to rid your life of alcohol completely. Alcohol is all around us, so part of your recovery is going to involve learning how to deal with this. But, if you have friends that you associate only with drinking, then you may need to cut them out of your life.

Friends Or Drinking Buddies

One of the hardest things that you will have to do when you get sober is noticing who your real friends are and who are simply your drinking buddies. For years you have been surrounding yourself with others who share your enthusiasm for drinking because they didn't judge you. When you first get sober, you may find that you feel lonely. At first, you might find it disconcerting, but after a while, you will start to figure the difference between your real friends and your drinking buddies.

Hanging out with your drinking buddies is extremely dangerous for a newly sober person. Typically, you can only relate to them in terms of alcohol. They may try to talk you into doing things that will cost you your sobriety. They may try to tell you that you can drink just one, or drink in moderation. You know that you can't stop at just one, but their arguments could sway you into trying it.

Most of the time, they don't even realize the dangers of the things they are saying. They think that the treatment you have gone through and your sobriety has fixed your problem and that you can be a social drinker. For others, they could have started to realize they have a drinking problem now that you have become sober and they don't want to be sober, which causes them to project their fears onto you.

How To Stop Drinking Alcohol Today

Before you decide to confront a drinking buddy to cut them out of your life, you should wait until you have reached a strong point in your recovery. Simply being around them could trigger a relapse.

The following are some helpful hints that you can use to end a friendship if you find that you need to:

- Let it simply run its course. You can gradually start to reduce your interactions with that person over time. This is usually a non-confrontational and peaceful way to end a friendship. Eventually, both people will feel that the relationship is simply phased out.

- Try to stay away from hostility. This is a hard situation as it is, and adding extra hostility to it is only going to make things worse. Be kind, and don't forget about your friend's feelings as well.

- Be completely honest with them and be direct. If you can't simply phase out the relationship, talk directly to them. Be honest about what is going on and explain to them the reason why you are ending the relationship. Explain that it is for your own good. This may be tough to say and hard for them to hear, but somebody who cares will understand and support your decision.

If your friends end up lashing out or become upset, there is a good chance that they were never a good friend to begin with. If you do choose to stay friends with drinkers, stay away from situations and places where alcohol use is likely to occur.

When you become sober, you will soon realize the people you can count on. These are people who are excited for you and are willing to help you maintain your sobriety. They want to support you. Part of your reason you chose to give up alcohol is so that you could become healthier and happier. This is going to help you to make close friends and strengthen the friendships you care about. Your friends will do whatever they can to help you. Knowing that you have people who care about you will help you in your sobriety.

If you choose to go to meetings, which I truly hope you do, it will open you up to a whole community of people who can become your friends and help you stay sober. You will discover that you aren't alone, and these people will be able to give you more support than your family and friends.

Dealing With Being Sober

You will find yourself in situations where you may be the only sober person in the room. You could be invited to a wedding or some party where drinking is involved. This is life and will happen from time to time. You can't keep yourself locked away for the rest of your life. You can still go out and have fun without drinking.

Let's take a look at some tips to make sure that you keep your sobriety and have fun at the same time:

How To Stop Drinking Alcohol Today

1. Out It

As a newly sober person, lying is probably something that you have left behind with the alcohol. You used to lie about drinking, but now you don't have to. So be honest in these social situations. People may give you an odd look if you choose lemon water instead of a cocktail, so own it. This will help you feel empowered. Show them that you don't care if your sobriety surprises them or makes them uncomfortable. You are sober and they drink. That's that. Stand strong in who you are.

2. Get Ready to Answer Questions

Besides getting some stares, people could become curious. Most people know that sober people surround themselves with sober people, so you are kind of a unicorn. People may start asking you why you are sober, especially if you are willing to answer these questions.

How To Stop Drinking Alcohol Today

A common question you may get is, "Were you that bad?" This is a very subjective question, so it will probably be tough to answer. A good way to answer it is, "I was bad enough that I had to quit." It's true, and if said in the right way, might get a bit of a laugh.

You may also hear things like, "You are never going to drink ever again?" "Don't you miss it?" and "You can't even drink sometimes?" It might start feeling like they are trying to prove that you aren't some scary stereotype. The media is to blame for this problem. They have long made alcoholics and hard drugs users look like terrible people that you should never be around.

3. Be There for a Good Reason

This is the most important thing to remember. If you are going to be someplace where alcohol is served, make sure you want to be there and that you will enjoy the company of the people around you. Maybe you chose to go to a concert of your favorite band.

How To Stop Drinking Alcohol Today

Whatever it is, the more you actually want to be there, the easier it will be to keep from drinking.

Being sober is no longer about going someplace just to go. It's about doing things that you want. Doing things that alcohol has caused you to miss out on. You are there for the company and entertainment, not for the drinks.

4. Take Comfort in Sobriety

Look at it this way, you aren't going to have to figure who is going to drive you home. You are always going to be able to drive, and you know that you are going to wake up in your own bed and know exactly what you did the day before.

5. Remind Yourself Why

When you get scared about the fact that you may be the only sober person around, remind yourself why you chose to be sober. You made an extremely hard decision to make your life healthier. You are a confident and sober person. This is no easy task, and it is something that you have to remind yourself of every single day.

When you are newly sober, these things can be the scariest things you have to face. With time, you will learn how to handle these times. You will also have more real friends that you can lean on for help.

Creating New Habits Of Distraction

While we have already covered the fact that alcoholism isn't a habit but a disease, you can still use the same strategies to break a bad habit to help distract yourself from the desire to drink.

Drinking has been disrupting your life for a while and has kept you from accomplishing your goals. It has put your health at risk, both physically and mentally. And it has completely wasted your energy and time.

By giving it up, you have created free time in your day to do things you have never had the chance to do. This is a good time to start something new. It's time to make a new habit.

There are four steps to building a habit: Cue, crave, response, and reward. When you break down these stages, you can understand what exactly a habit is and the best way to create one.

Cue

This is what cues your brain to initiate your new habit. When you drank, this cue could have been getting home from work, going out, or a Friday night. The prehistoric man paid attention to cues that meant that there were rewards like water, food, or sex. Today, most of our cues predict secondary rewards like power, fame, money, approval, praise, and love

The mind is continuously looking through your internal and external environment for where rewards may be. Since the cue is your first indication that you are close to a reward, it will lead to a craving.

Craving

The second stage of a habit loop is cravings, and these cravings are what motivates us to act on our habit. Without some sort of desire, we have no reason to act. When you drank, the motivation was the feeling you got from the alcohol. The thing that you crave isn't the actual habit, but what it gives. As a drinker, you don't crave the drink; you crave the feeling that it provides you. You aren't motivated by running, but the sense of accomplishment you get after. Each craving has a link to some desire to change your current state.

Cravings will differ for everybody. In theory, any type of information could end up triggering a craving, but in reality, everybody is motivated by different cues. For a gambler, it could the chime of the slot machines. Cues are completely meaningless until the brain interprets them.

Response

This is the part where you actually perform the habit. The response depends on how motivated you are. If there is an action that is going to require a lot of mental and physical effort, then you will likely avoid it. The response also depends on ability.

Reward

This is what you get from your habit. Your cue was noticing what the reward was. The craving is wanting that reward. The response is getting the reward. We want these rewards for two reasons: One, they teach us, and, two, they satisfy us.

Rewards teach us that our actions are worth remembering. The brain works on a system of rewards. Your senses will be on a constant lookout for similar situations.

Rewards also satisfy our cravings. While rewards can benefit us in some ways, it is the immediate reward that our brains are on the lookout for.

Creating A New Habit

Now let's see how you can create a new habit so that you can forget about drinking:

1. Think of something new that you can do instead

How To Stop Drinking Alcohol Today

If you want to create a habit on times where you would normally end up drinking, you will need to figure out when you have your cravings. When you would normally want a drink, you could choose to do some breathing exercises.

2. Get rid of as many triggers as you can

This could be as simple as throwing out the alcohol you have in your house. If you tend to drink when you go out to eat, maybe skip going out for a while.

3. Get somebody to join you

Doing things with other people is always easier. Find somebody else to do this with you.

4. Find a mentor

Find others that are living a life that you would like to live and become their friends. They can help guide you in your new habits.

How To Stop Drinking Alcohol Today

Remember, you want to keep the same cue you have before; you are simply changing the actual habit to something that is healthier than drinking.

Alcoholics Anonymous

One of the best ways to get help as an alcoholic is through Alcoholics Anonymous. AA is an international group of men and women who all suffer from a drinking problem. These groups are apolitical, multiracial, self-supporting, nonprofessional, and available almost everywhere. There aren't any educational nor age requirements. Anybody who wants support for their drinking problem is welcome to join.

AA was founded in 1935 by Dr. Bob and Bill W. in Akron, Ohio. The program grew from two alcoholics meeting up on June 10 1935, when the book *Alcoholics Anonymous* was published. This is what is known as "The Big Book". Then, another article was published in 1941 in the *Saturday Evening Post*.

Memberships

Drug and alcohol addiction is sometimes called a "chemical dependency" or "substance abuse." Alcoholics and non-alcoholics alike are sometimes introduced to AA and urged to start attending meetings. Anybody is allowed to attend open AA meetings.

If a meeting is open, then it is open for the public to come. There are closed meetings that only members can attend. Only people who have a drinking problem can go to closed meetings and become an AA member. People who suffer from other problems can only be eligible for AA if they suffer from a drinking problem as well.

AA traditions state that the only qualifications they require for membership is a desire to quit drinking.

Since 12-step groups are based on the fact of anonymity, meetings are typically closed in order to protect their privacy. Members have the freedom of going, knowing that everybody there are all guided by the traditions and steps of the group, which encourages all of them to maintain their anonymity and other members' anonymity.

Closed meetings are where members are able to speak honestly and openly about all of their situations or problems, knowing that everybody in the room have gone through similar things.

Open meetings mean that visitors, and possibly the media, can be present and members will normally conduct themselves according to this. Not always, but most open meetings will have a special speaker. This person is the designated speaker of the meeting, sharing their own story. They have been informed before the meeting that it is open and non-members may be present. Sharing typically doesn't happen in meetings with guest speakers.

Open meetings are meant to give people a chance to see what the program is about and decide whether or not they want to become a member. When you are looking for a meeting, the schedule will usually show if it is open or closed. If it does not state which it is, you should consider it to be closed.

What AA Can Do for You

In AA, members share stories about things they have gone through to help other people who need help with a drinking problem. Most everybody in AA gets a sponsor with the first meeting or so to have a person who can give them one-on-one support. Alcoholics Anonymous is a 12-step program and provides the alcoholic a way to create a life without alcohol. This program is explained in meetings.

Typically, closed AA meetings will have a topic for discussion. The person that leads the meeting will pick a topic and members will share their experience on that particular thing. There are some meetings that are meant for a certain purpose, like beginners' meetings or 12-step study groups.

How To Stop Drinking Alcohol Today

People will likely have their own misconceptions about AA meetings because of how they are portrayed on TV. Don't let this deter you from going and seeing for yourself what they are all about.

What to Expect

There are a lot of beliefs people have about AA, but many of these are myths. For example:

- You may recognize people

- You are joining a cult

- You must pray

- You have to be a part of group hugs

- You have to share everything about your addiction

- You have to say, "I am an alcoholic"

- You are going to be surrounded by "helpful" alcoholics

How To Stop Drinking Alcohol Today

The truth is, the meeting may help in a place like a community center or a church meeting room. There will be other people there for the meeting and some people will be making coffee and setting up snacks. There will be some people who will introduce themselves and others that keep to themselves.

Once the meeting begins, everybody will sit in a semi-circle with one person in the middle – the chairperson for that meeting.

It starts by the chairperson reading the AA Preamble and then they will recite the Serenity Prayer. Typically, around 80% of the people recite the prayer. This means that if you don't pray, you don't have to. Don't let this discourage you.

Then, people will read different AA literature and the chairperson will ask if there are any newcomers who want to introduce themselves. There may be some who raise their hand. If you want to, then do so.

How To Stop Drinking Alcohol Today

If this is a step meeting, the chairperson will say which step you will be discussing. They will read the step chapter, and then the chairperson will ask if somebody has anything to share that relates to that share.

With sharing, everybody will start with "Hello, my name is (first name), and I'm an alcoholic." And as with the movies, everybody will say, "Hello (first name)." They will then share and thank everybody once they are finished.

Once people have finished sharing, the chairperson will ask if there are any announcements that are AA related. Then everybody will stand in a circle, hold hands, and say The Lord's Prayer. Nobody is required to participate in this prayer; you can simply stand in the circle and show support. After the prayer ends, the meeting is over.

Afterwards, some people may socialize or go get something to eat with other members. You do what you feel is good for you.

How To Stop Drinking Alcohol Today

Don't worry about being forced to do things that you don't want to. You don't have to share and you don't have to have religious views even though they recite prayers. Nobody will force you into doing these things.

12 Steps

While you will learn more about these in an actual meeting, here are the steps and a basic explanation of what they are. An actual meeting can guide you through these:

1. Honesty – After years of denial, recovery can only start when you admit that you are powerless over alcohol.

2. Faith –A higher power can only help if you believe that it can. This can be any higher power, not just God. The main thing is that you believe there is something greater than you.

3. Surrender – A lifetime of running can stop and be changed if you make the decision to hand it over to something higher than you.

4. Soul Searching – One thing you will hear in these meetings is that it is a process, not an event; the same is true for this step. You will learn more about yourself.

5. Integrity – This may be the hardest step of all, but it also gives you the most growth.

6. Acceptance – You have to accept there are flaws in you and everything that you can't change.

7. Humility – Willing to accept the fact you can't do everything yourself and asking for help when you need it.

8. Willingness – This is making amends to people whom you have harmed through your addiction.

9. Forgiveness – Amends may be hard, but for those who want help, this is the perfect medicine.

10. Maintenance – You have to be willing to admit when you are wrong in order to maintain your sobriety.

11. Making Contact – This is discovering your higher power's plan for you.

12. Service – This is "how it works."

Effectiveness

Because of the confidential nature of AA where the members practice anonymity and all of the traditions of AA which discourages the members from helping "outside enterprises," there aren't very many studies on how effective AA is. However, there are a lot of studies about how people in mutual support groups have better odds of staying sober after three years than people who tried to do it on their own.

Is It Right For You?

Obviously, faith-based programs like AA aren't the right choice for everybody. While there are millions who say that they have found recovery through AA, the spiritual part of the program tends to be a problem for some. The only way to know whether or not it is for you, and if you can get past the spiritual aspect, if that is a problem, is to go to a meeting.

It is effective for most, so it is worth the time to see if you can make it work for you. AA is free to use, so you have nothing to lose.

To find a meeting, you can go to the AA website, or you can flip through the white pages. Most white pages will have the number for local meetings. You can call them and find out when the next open meeting is. You can also join through online meetings as well.

Part Two: The Scientific Approach

The Sinclair Method

The Sinclair Method (TSM) is a more scientific approach to treating alcohol addiction. It uses what is known as "pharmacological extinction". They use an opiate blocker to erase habit-forming behaviors. The effects of this will change a person's alcohol addiction to what it was before they were addicted.

TSM requires a person to take either Nalmefene or Naltrexone at least an hour before they have their first drink and for the remainder of their life, or as long as they choose to drink. Naltrexone chemically changes how the body reacts to the behavior/reward cycle, which makes you want to drink less.

Studies on the Sinclair Method have proven that it is equally effective with or without some form of therapy. This means that patients can decide whether or not they want to combine it with therapy. The actual results are going to be the same, although the extinction will happen around month three or four. About a quarter of people on TSM will become 100 percent alcohol-free. For those who decide not to stop drinking, they will continue to have to take the medicine before they start drinking for as long as they choose to continue to use alcohol.

The Sinclair Method was developed by Dr. John D. Sinclair. Unlike many other treatment methods that require a person to completely give up alcohol, this method lets them continue drinking. In fact, success is dependent on continued consumption with the use of Naltrexone.

When Naltrexone is taken before drinking, it blocks the endorphins that are released when a person consumes alcohol. When these endorphins are blocked, a person doesn't receive a rewarding experience. This means that you don't get the pleasure of drinking, which causes you to drink in excess.

Over time, the brain will unlearn the association between alcohol and pleasure. This will reduce cravings and will improve your control over your alcohol use.

Abstinence Isn't Required

Following the Sinclair Method does not require you to give up drinking altogether if that is not your goal. Some people will find it awkward to totally give up drinking because they don't feel like they can go and do things with their friends because drinking will inevitably be involved. They know if they were to drink in these situations, they will likely end up losing control.

The Sinclair Method will allow you to participate in these customs as long as you make sure you take Naltrexone at least an hour before your first drink. This will allow you to control how much you drink.

How To Stop Drinking Alcohol Today

It could be that you stop at one, or you have a couple, but your decision will be appropriate for the event. You could also decide to have no drinks, if that is what you want.

The theory behind the Sinclair Method is that being told you have to completely abstain from alcohol causes you to become more preoccupied with drinking and intensifies cravings. This is what is referred to as the "alcohol deprivation effect".

The brain is dependent on alcohol, and will not rest until it gets a taste of alcohol. This is why AA members have to continue going for the rest of their lives. You may not have had a drink in ten years, but your brain is still addicted to alcohol.

AA will even teach that if you have been sober for 20 years and you slip, you will start drinking exactly where you left off. Abstinence doesn't change the neurobiology of addiction. That being said, you should not be discouraged if you choose to go the non-drug route to become sober. There are millions of people who are sober simply through abstinence and therapy. You don't have to follow the Sinclair Method to be successful.

People who relapse after abstaining from alcohol tend to do so in a self-destructive binge. This is normally characterized by large quantities of alcohol, more than what was used before.

The reason that this happens is because of a neurological disorder that was created after the brain has been trained to associate drinking with pleasure. This is what is known as "operant conditioning", which is a form of learning. The brain has learned that alcohol equals pleasure.

Through pharmacological extinction, you can un-learn this pattern when you use Naltrexone because your brain is eventually no longer going to associate alcohol with pleasure. Your brain is going to end up losing interest in alcohol, and you will discover that you can simply take it or leave it.

Abstinence doesn't teach this to your brain. You simply learn how to cope with your cravings and find new ways to give your brain that endorphin fix.

Dr. John D. Sinclair

Dr. Sinclair was an American doctor who began studying alcoholism in lab animals and people during the late 70s. His work was mainly done in Finland where receive a lot of support.

He came up with the theory that alcoholism is a learned behavior, similar to a Pavlovian conditioning. Drinking creates pleasure, even though in reality it actually just takes way discomfort, and this is seen as pleasurable. Each time that a person takes a drink, this belief is reinforced. Later on, once a physical dependency is formed, a similar occurrence begins to happen.

This anticipation for pleasure is the controlling factor. Drinking removes jitters, and this is seen as pleasurable, even though it doesn't actually create any true pleasure. We all know that all it is doing is feeding the cycle.

The main reason, according to Dr. Sinclair, that Naltrexone hasn't found more use is that it often gets used incorrectly.

It is an odd medication and has the ability to affect any act that releases endorphins. This means that if it is taken incorrectly, it can cause a loss of pleasure in exercise, eating, sex, or any anything else that is seen as pleasurable, and this causes people to stop doing these activities.

This is why you should only take Naltrexone an hour before you know for certain that you are going to drink, and only on the days that you know you will be drinking. If used in this way, in about a month's time, your alcohol consumption will be greatly decreased, or you will have stopped altogether. When taken correctly, the medication will start to recondition the brain and its need for alcohol.

The FDA authorized the use of Naltrexone by the mid-90s, but they said the alcoholic should take the medication every day and abstain from drinking alcohol. During clinical trials, this didn't have as much success as the placebo group. However, some did see success. As it turned out, those who saw success had cheated and drank anyway.

Dr. Sinclair believed that the medication had to actually interact with the drinking behavior in order to be successful. To experience decreasing pleasure in drinking, you have to drink. Without drinking while taking the medicine, it only increased the craving. Worse yet, by abstaining and taking the medicine, the medicine would end up interacting with all experiences that were seen as pleasurable, or any act that released endorphins. This caused life to seem bland.

The Risk

While the correct use of this drug has seen positive results, there are variables that can cause some problems. First off, drinking is dangerous for alcoholics. Ten percent of people who took this medication didn't show a positive response. Another ten percent couldn't follow the directions correctly in order to benefit from it. Of the other 80% that would go on to see positive results, the initial phase still had potential risk. During the early phase of use, the medication didn't affect them that much, and drinking is just as risky, or more so, as it would have been if they weren't taking the medication.

Even after the medication began to take effect, but while their drinking was still heavy, it was only the pleasurable effects of alcohol that is reduced. The effect on judgment, social interactions, reaction time, and motor skills are still as strong as they would be without the medication. This means that there is still a chance for problematic outcomes during the first couple of weeks of use.

This means that doctors are hesitant to recommend that person "drink themselves sober." Insurance companies are also reluctant to accept this treatment form. For those who have already taken the sober route, they should not think that they can start taking this so that they can go enjoy a drink. This can be very dangerous and pointless because they have already reached abstinence and do not need to risk a relapse.

The biggest risk, though, is the long-term efficacy of the Sinclair Method, especially if this is the only thing a person has used to help their drinking. The problem is that a person can become too lax in taking the medication.

For whatever reason, if a person forgets to take Naltrexone before they drink, it is going to cause them problems. They have the potential of relearning their drinking behavior. Patients who choose to use the Sinclair Method must make sure that they keep Naltrexone with them at all times so that they can take it an hour before they take their first drink.

How To Stop Drinking Alcohol Today

In the end, going to AA meetings for the rest of your life is no different than making sure you take Naltrexone for the rest of your life. There haven't been any studies done to see if the effectiveness of using these two methods together is any better than doing one or the other. Also, the chance of relapse for both is just as likely, but missing a single AA meeting isn't likely to cause you to relapse like forgetting to take Naltrexone before you drink will.

In the end, it is up to you as to how you choose to get sober. Continue reading about other prescription methods of controlling alcohol use.

Naltrexone And Other Prescription Help

There are just three medicines that have been approved by the United States Food and Drug Administration to treat alcohol abuse. None of these will be prescribed to anyone who is still drinking. These are for people who have stopped drinking and are trying to remain sober.

There aren't any medications out there for people who are still drinking that will make them stop.

Naltrexone

Naltrexone helps with alcohol cravings. It works by blocking the area of the brain that causes the "high" that you experience when drinking. You will feel drunk but you won't feel any pleasure that you used to feel when getting drunk.

Naltrexone was developed in 1963 to treat opioid addiction. The FDA approved it in 1984 to treat drugs like oxycodone, morphine, and heroin. During this time it was sold using the name "Trexan" by DuPont.

During the 80s, studies on animals found that Naltrexone could reduce alcohol consumption. Human trials soon followed during the late 80s and into the early 90s. These trials found that when it was added to psychosocial therapies, it could reduce cravings and this decreased the relapse rates among alcoholics.

In 1994, the FDA approved Naltrexone to be used to treat alcoholism. DuPont renamed it "Revia" at this point.

Disulfiram

This drug also goes by the name "Antabuse". It is used as a deterrent to drinking. Disulfiram was the first medication to be approved by the FDA to be used to treat alcohol dependency and abuse. It works by creating a severe reaction when somebody takes the medicine and then drinks alcohol. Many people who take it will begin vomiting after they drink alcohol. This is supposed to make them not want to drink again. When you begin associating alcohol with sweating, headaches, vomiting, nausea, and a hangover like you've never experienced before, you aren't going to want anything at all to do with alcohol.

Disulfiram was created in the 20s to be used in manufacturing processes. The reactions of disulfiram were first found during the 30s. People who worked in a vulcanized rubber industry who were constantly exposed to tetraethylthiuram disulfide got sick after they drank alcohol.

During 1948, researchers in Denmark were trying to find a treatment for infections caused by a parasite. They discovered the alcohol effects of Disulfiram when they got sick after they drank alcohol. These researchers started a new study about using Disulfiram to treat the dependence on alcohol.

Shortly afterwards, the United States Food and Drug Administration approved Disulfiram as a way to treat alcoholism. Wyeth-Ayerst Laboratories first manufactured the drug under the name "Antabuse".

At first, Disulfiram was given in large dosages to create aversion conditioning. It made people extremely sick when they drank. After several reported severe reactions that included a few deaths, Antabuse was given in smaller dosages to help support abstinence from alcohol.

Acamprosate

Acamprosate is also known by the name "Campral". It is the most recent medicine that has been approved to treat alcohol dependency in the United States. It helps alcoholics by reducing the emotional discomfort and physical distress that people experience once they stop drinking – symptoms like depression, restlessness, anxiety, and insomnia that could last for several months after one has stopped drinking.

Acamprosate works by making two chemical messengers in the brain interact: glutamate and GABA, which stands for gamma-aminobutyric acid. If GABA is working right, it will stifle specific nerve cells to help control anxiety and fear that you feel when these cells get overexcited. Glutamate actually stimulates nerve cells.

One big disadvantage of this drug is that you have to take two pills three times a day. If you have problems swallowing pills, you can't remember to take pills, or you already have too much medicine to take, this medication might be a bit hard for you.

During 1982, a French company called "Laboratoires Meram" created Acamprosate to treat alcohol dependency. They tested it for efficacy and safety from the years 1982 to 1988. The French governments authorized its use in 1988 to treat alcoholism. They marketed it under the name of "Aotal".

For about 20 years, Acamprosate was used all over Europe to treat alcohol abuse. The United States didn't approve its use until July of 2004. The United States marketed this drug in January 2005 under the name of "Campral".

Campral is still being marketed in the US by Forest Pharmaceuticals. Just like Naltrexone, this works best for anybody who can stop drinking before they start treatment.

Other Medications

There are two other medications, Topiramate, and Gabapentin that interact with the glutamate and GABA systems. The FDA has approved these to help treat seizures. Some doctors have prescribed them to be used to help alcoholism.

Studies that have been done show that they could help people have fewer cravings, drink less, and stay away from drinking.

Gabapentin is the new kid in the defense of alcoholism but it is showing some great results. It is being used to treat alcoholism in other countries at this point. The FDA hasn't approved it to be used for this purpose yet.

Long Term Results

There is a lot of research being done about the effects of taking medicines for longer than one year. The benefits of longer use aren't clear.

The main question might be: "Is medicine alone enough to stop someone from drinking?" They can take the medicine but if they don't change their behavior, nothing is really going to change. Medication might just be as good as a person's motivation to recover.

How To Stop Drinking Alcohol Today

How a person achieves a behavior changes will vary from person to person. Psychotherapy and counseling could help some. Others might need regular visits to their doctor.

Researchers haven't compared psychotherapy alone to medication but the results are very mixed. It isn't known if combining them will give better benefits than just using them alone. Other studies show that just getting help, whether it is through counseling, medicines or both is what is needed to successfully manage alcoholism.

Life After Naltrexone

The amount of time you are on Naltrexone all depends on the plan that you and your doctor come up with. Many people will take it for 12 weeks or longer. Research has shown that taking it for longer than three months is the best treatment. Make sure that you take the Naltrexone the way your doctor told you to. Never take any more than what the prescription says. Never skip any doses. Never stop taking the pill unless you speak with your doctor first.

If you don't like the thought of taking a pill every day, there are different types of Naltrexone. All forms have the same effects.

- Tablet

This is the type of Naltrexone that is used in a rehab facility. Tablet can be sold under the names of Depade and ReVia and are normally taken once daily. Tablets are the most prescribed type but it is hard to remember to take a pill at the exact same time each day. If you miss a dose, or you take more than is prescribed, there are some health problems that could happen.

- Injectable

There are some rehab centers and in-patient facilities that will give Naltrexone as a shot. This form is sold under the name of "Vivitrol". It is injected into muscle just once a month. Patients could experience redness, swelling, pain, or tenderness at the injection site for a couple of days after the injection. This is a good alternative to having to remember to take a pill each day. It is very important to keep a consistent schedule when using this type of Naltrexone. You have to take this once every four weeks. This is a good alternative for anyone who has problems swallowing a pill.

- Implant

This is the newest form of Naltrexone that is used in clinics and rehab facilities. A small implant gets inserted under the skin. This will slowly release the medicine into the body for about eight weeks. Because this option doesn't require any attention, it is great for anybody who receives treatment from an outpatient center. The bad news is that some insurance won't cover the cost for this device. You must check with your insurance before you decide if you want this type of Naltrexone.

Am I Going to Need Other Treatments, Too?

Just like any other disease, alcoholism will affect you mentally and physically. Your mind and body both need to be treated. Your doctor might recommend that you go for some psychosocial treatments. This type of treatment might help you cope with your problems and change your behavior. Some examples of this type of treatment could include:

- Hospital stay

- Addiction treatment programs

- Group therapy

- Family therapy

- Counseling

- Support groups

- Alcoholics Anonymous

There might be some centers in the area that offer these treatments. Your doctor will be able to refer you to the right psychosocial treatment center.

Side Effects

Just like any other medicine, there are possible side effects that you need to be aware of. Some of these side effects might be mild and will only last a couple of days but others might be a lot more serious. If you have alcohol in your system, it can make these side effects a lot worse and could cause other health problems.

Here are the most common side effects:

- Nausea

- Restlessness

- Anxiety

- Insomnia

- Headaches

- Stomach cramps

- Vomiting

- Joint or muscle pain

- Diarrhea

- Dizziness

- Drowsiness

- Nervousness

- Constipation

If you experience any of these side effects, let your doctor know. They might change your treatment plan or give you some suggestions on ways you can deal with these side effects.

There are some rare side effects that are very serious. If you have any of the following symptoms, call your doctor immediately.

- Severe diarrhea

- Severe vomiting

- Hallucinations

- Confusion

- Blurry vision

- Depression

- Tinnitus or ringing of the ears

- Swelling in the legs, feet or face

- Shortness of breath

Things to Know Before Starting Naltrexone

Naltrexone isn't normally prescribed after the first year of treatment since it isn't intended to be used long term. Before you take Naltrexone, you need to talk with your doctor about all the above side effects. Make sure you tell them about any over the counter or prescription medications that you are already taking. Since some medicines could cause serious reactions if combined with Naltrexone, you absolutely must talk with your doctor or treatment specialist before taking them.

Naltrexone blocks the areas of the brain where alcohol and narcotics work. You need to be careful to not take any narcotics while on Naltrexone. Narcotics include heroin, morphine, or codeine. Never take cough syrup that has codeine in it while taking Naltrexone. If you take narcotics, Naltrexone can make withdrawal symptoms worse. You have to stop taking narcotics at least seven to ten days before starting Naltrexone.

If you are pregnant, never take Naltrexone. Talk to your doctor about other birth control options. It isn't known if Naltrexone gets into breast milk, so never breastfeed when taking Naltrexone.

Questions For Your Doctor

Here are some questions you should ask your doctor before starting Naltrexone:

- What will happen if I take drugs while taking Naltrexone?

- I want to stop being an alcoholic. Will Naltrexone help me?

- Will I get drunk if I drink alcohol while taking Naltrexone?

- Can I drink while taking Naltrexone?

- What are some possible side effects?

Deciding to get help for your alcoholism will be the biggest decision of your life. It is important to know that not all rehab centers are the same. Most programs will focus on certain addictions and offer certain therapies.

Ending the Cycle

When you are choosing a rehab center, know what aspects are most important to you. Ask the admission's person these questions to see what their treatment includes:

- What do you do on a normal day here?

- Which addictions do you treat?

- Does your program offer treatments that are ongoing like counseling and support groups?

- Which medicines do you use during the detox period and into continued treatment?

- Does your facility help people transition back into normal life once rehab is over?

- Which therapies do your specialists use, and are they effective?

Nobody ever has to suffer in silence from alcoholism. If you want to start on your journey to recovery, there is help out there. Find a rehab center or specialist to get the help you need.

Keeping Track Of Your Progress

When you were younger, you might have kept a diary or journal. You know that being able to write down your feelings and thoughts helped you get to know yourself better and you were able to process some hard emotions. Writing in a journal can be good for your mental health, but it can be very helpful when you are dealing with the challenges of recovery from alcoholism.

Many people who are in recovery and trying to remain sober keep a journal. Keeping a journal is a great way to get thoughts out of your head and to process feelings. Sometimes problems won't seem as awful or huge when you can work them out on paper.

By keeping a journal, you will be able to watch your progress as you move from being an alcoholic to being sober. In a year or so, you can look back at what you wrote and it might amaze you at all the

87

things you accomplished. You will be so proud of yourself.

Your journal doesn't need to be anything fancy. You can make a journal out of a binder and notebook paper. You could email thoughts to yourself, find an app, or begin a file on your computer. You get to write about anything you want. Nobody has to see what you write, so be honest.

You might not know what you should write in your journal. It is your journal; you get to write anything you want. Here are some thoughts to get you started:

- Your dreams and hopes for your future

- Reflections about your progress

- Long and short term goals

- Thoughts about your eating habits along with foods you want to try

How To Stop Drinking Alcohol Today

- Relaxation and meditation practices you would like to try

- How you see yourself

- Your progress and victories during recovery

- Work problems and thoughts about your finances

- Your weaknesses and strengths

- What motivates you to remain sober

- What are your priorities now

- Ways you can fix your relationships

- How you make amends to everyone

- How you will react when you run into former friends

- What are you grateful for

- How you will avoid triggers

How To Stop Drinking Alcohol Today

- How you will deal with cravings

- Triggers that you know of

- How you feel after a therapy session

- How you feel after an AA meeting

- Your recovery plan

- How do you feel about being sober

- What are you feeling today

These are just to get you started and you don't even have to use any of the above topics. They are there for when you just can't come up with anything to write about. Journaling is very individualized. You get to focus on whatever you want to in order to help keep you sober. Once you have gotten into the habit of keeping a daily journal, you will be reinforcing the concept of living life day-by-day. You will be able to process and deal with problems as they happen instead of them getting blown out of proportion.

Benefits of Keeping a Journal

There are many benefits to writing in a journal. It is a way to understand your past, present and your future. The most wonderful benefit of journaling is the mental clarity that you experience when you document your experiences during sobriety. It doesn't matter if your experiences are overwhelming or ordinary. When you write them down, it could help you process your feelings along with how you react to these experiences, both good and bad.

- Understanding Yourself

Writing in a journal helps you understand yourself better. The longer you keep a journal and the more you write in your journal, you might notice some triggers or patterns that make you want to drink. You might begin to see things that make you feel excited to be sober and alive. You could also see specific types of self-talk that is negative and might threaten your sobriety. If you can recognize these thoughts, it

91

can allow you to find a way to reframe them from a positive viewpoint. Problems are staying stuck in your head and any bad experiences won't get blown up. They are written down and then sorted through.

When you write in a journal, you get to release your deepest, darkest secrets and feelings. This is important for when you have feelings of despair and sadness or when you are full of joy and elation. If you feel frustrated or unhappy, writing these things down allows you to release negative emotions and vent. Don't hold anything back since nobody will be seeing what you are writing. If you keep negative feelings inside, it could threaten your sobriety; being able to write about your emotions is healing. Your journal is a safe place where you can let your feelings out without being criticized or judged.

- Seeing Progress

If you are new to sobriety, you are probably sorting through some confusing emotions. This is where your journal comes into play. Write down all these emotions in your journal and in time, you will notice that things will begin to make sense. You will find that you are getting better at dealing with challenges. Your entries will show the positive changes in chronological order, showing your road to success.

While moving forward in your sobriety, your journal will act as an inspiration about how far you have come. If you have some spare time, take some time and read back over your journal from the very start and you might be surprised at how far you have come.

- Keeping Your Privacy

There is another benefit of keeping a journal and that is you get to keep your feelings and thoughts completely private. You get to be as honest and raw as you want. If you would like to write about your challenges or experiences of dealing with craving and triggers, go for it. Nobody is going to read your journal or judge anything you write. No need to worry about grammar or spelling since nobody is going to see it. You also have the option of keeping your journal as audio files.

If you are worried that somebody might find your journal and then violate your privacy, if you are writing your journal on your computer, protect the file with a password. If your journal is on paper, find a safe place that only you know about to keep it.

The musician Nick Murphy describes how he benefited from keeping a journal in a powerful but simple way. He stated that writing in his journal served that same purpose that running or walking gave him. They were physical means to clear out his mental landscape.

If you have any pent-up feelings that are very hard for you to process, keeping a journal can be your safe place to release these emotions while staying sober. Don't worry about how much or what you should write about in one session. There isn't a wrong or right way of keeping a journal. Just put your pen against paper and watch where it leads you.

Types of Journaling

You have many different choices when journaling. The easiest way to journal is writing about what you experience daily. Did you have lunch with anyone? Did you experience any feelings? Writing about your day will help you sort through all that mental clutter and come out with peace and clarity.

With paper, you will be able to express your deepest feelings just like you would with a dear friend. You can set a time when you want to write for a specific amount of time. This way, you can just write about whatever enters your mind. It doesn't have to make sense. You can write about what is happening right this moment, or just random thoughts.

Another journal is a gratitude journal. In this journal, you write down between three and five things that you are grateful for daily. It is hard to remain angry or scared when you are focusing on being grateful. Writing in a gratitude journal will help you pay attention to all the positive things that have happened to you during your day.

Journaling And Recovery

Keeping a journal is a great sobriety tool. When you write in your journal, you can be totally honest. If you like, you could write about your addiction and the way you are able to handle stressful situations now without drinking. You can write about how much you feel like drinking without actually acting upon it. It is a good idea to take the focus off cravings and write about other experiences that you want to have one day.

Your journal is a record of your sobriety progress, and with some time, you might be amazed to see exactly how far you have come. Early in your sobriety, you might see that what you wrote in your journal was just a bunch of tangled emotions and confusion. As time passes, your life will begin to make sense. You will be able to see that you are better at dealing with life on its terms, and you may also realize that journaling is playing a huge role in helping your sobriety.

What If I Relapse?

Anyone who goes through rehab will hear these six words: Relapse is a part of recovery. In many ways, this statement is very dangerous. It sounds like a relapse is unavoidable and since it is, it has to be fine.

Well, I'm here to tell you that it isn't.

A relapse is not unavoidable and it isn't ever fine. It will put everything that you have worked so hard for at risk: Your future, rebuilding your life, and your sobriety.

A better way to phrase this idea would be: Finding the best way to deal with relapse will be part of your recovery.

This is a subtle difference but it is very real. This statement addresses the relapse being a certainty but more of an obstacle that a person could overcome if they are committed to continuing their recovery.

How To Stop Drinking Alcohol Today

You might have tried to stop drinking but you have had a relapse. Not to worry, you aren't alone. Statistics say that about 90 percent of people who have tried to quit have had at least one relapse before they reached long-term sobriety.

There might be some cases where it was just a momentary lapse, which is called a slip. It is different than a full-blown relapse because the person immediately regrets what they have done. It could have been because of something that happened suddenly or if their focus was suddenly shaken. It will be characterized by the person wanting to immediately correct the mistake.

In contrast, a relapse would suggest that they have fallen back into their old behaviors. It is usually described when someone has been sober for a while goes back to drinking and won't be able to stop.

Why A Relapse Happens

Many people who are recovering from alcoholism don't start recovery because of their own free will. They are usually pressured into it by family and friends, told to by a judge, or they have hit what they consider to be "rock bottom."

Most of the time, alcoholics have other psychological or mental problems like PTSD, anxiety, or depression. The problems that these conditions cause won't magically go away when a person stops drinking.

If the two factors of concurrent disorders and initial reluctance get together in early recovery, they might cause the person who is still new to sobriety to be fragile and very susceptible to relapsing if they don't keep their environment structured in a way that is good for their sobriety.

Reasons For A Relapse

There are some cases where people slip because they don't have the tools available to overcome specific situations. They could have had a very bad day and will use this as an excuse to begin drinking again. They could become so overwhelmed by cravings that normally happen early on during the recovery period.

There might be other cases where a person uses alcohol to punish people around them for "making" them drink again. This lets them blame others instead of acknowledging that their addiction is their own problem.

The biggest point with a slip is that they will immediately regret their mistake. The problem happens when a simple slip becomes a complete relapse and they completely abandon their sobriety. If this were to happen, their ability to change things will be very hard for many reasons:

How To Stop Drinking Alcohol Today

- When they begin to drink again, they won't be able to make rational decisions.

- Their motivation to stay sober was very low to begin with and this makes it harder to try recovery again.

- A relapse often confirms to them that they won't ever be able to overcome their addiction.

- People who supported their recovery at first might not be willing to keep supporting them.

- Some people might try to fool themselves that they can get sober when things get better and that they are stronger.

- Others will try to tell themselves that they have to hit "rock bottom" before they can get completely sober. They don't understand that it's a trick to buy them some time to do the same things over again.

Other Factors That Causes A Relapse

In the early stages of recovery, an alcoholic who is new to sobriety might get overwhelmed when learning how to live this new life, cope with everyday stresses, and interact with other people.

The best way for a person to remain on course until the new lessons become second nature and ingrained in them is to create new habits that can be supported by structured, strong foundations. If you don't have this structure, you could be influenced in several ways:

- Not having any joy in life

Most people, during the early stages of their recovery, will experience depression while the chemistry of their brains tries to right itself. They are going to be miserable like they are mourning a loved one. In a way, they probably are since they don't have a relationship with alcohol anymore.

How To Stop Drinking Alcohol Today

- Being around the wrong people

It is impossible to remain sober if the people you spend time with are still getting drunk. Still associating with your old drinking buddies who still drink could make joining them very easy.

- No support system

This goes along with the one above. You have to distance yourself from people who could tempt you into drinking. You need to surround yourself with sober people who are positive and have your back. These need to be people that you feel comfortable talking to – people who can help shoulder your burdens when you start feeling overwhelmed. People who will nudge you in the direction you need to go to when you go off course.

- Being in the wrong places

How To Stop Drinking Alcohol Today

Being an alcoholic is a disease. If you continue to go to the same bars where you got drunk, you could begin repeating your old behaviors.

- Not going to meetings

When you have been sober for some time, you could begin feeling like you can handle your sobriety by yourself. The fact is that 12-step meetings along with regular therapy could bring you in contact with people who understand you. These people will give you inspiration and strength if you feel overwhelmed or tempted.

- Wrong things

Things? Basically, the way you used to cope and think. It was the old, unhealthy ways of doing stuff that caused your disease to get worse to begin with. Alcoholism is a disease of denial, stubbornness and ego. If you go back to your old responses, patterns, thoughts and behaviors, you are just wanting to fail.

How To Stop Drinking Alcohol Today

- Not having faith

At times, you won't be able to see the messages of recovery. You may not realize why a certain step or action is important and you might try some shortcuts. Recovery is a process. There might be times that you have to put your ego away and just trust the process that has worked for hundreds of people who were the same place you are at today.

- Not having patience

You might often feel frustrated when you aren't regaining back your life as fast as you thought you should. You are forgetting that you didn't develop this disease overnight. Recovery is going to take time.

- Doing too much

There is another mantra that you might hear during recover and this is: K.I.S.S. or Keep It Simple, Stupid. This just means that you need to focus more on your associations, activities, and actions that will help you recover. Don't try to heal each relationship and fix each mistake all at one time.

It doesn't matter what difficulties are present in your life. Living a life that is sober and clean will be so much better than an alcoholic's life that is spiraling out of control. You should be able to find joy when you realize this.

Does Relapsing Mean You Have Failed?

Seriously, no. Addiction is a disease, the same as hypertension, heart disease, and diabetes. Recovery is a learning process of making lifestyle changes that make your condition manageable. Here are some relapse rates for some health problems:

- 50 to 70 percent of the people who have asthma don't take their medicine regularly.

- 50 to 70 percent of people with hypertension don't comply with what their doctor's tell them.

- 30 to 60 percent of diabetics don't follow their exercise or diet plan.

- 40 to 60 percent of alcoholics will relapse.

In spite of the rate of noncompliance or relapse, nobody would ever tell a diabetic who indulged in a slice of pie that they have failed and need to just give up.

The Three Stages Of Alcohol Relapse

A relapse has three stages: physical, mental, and emotional. Here are some in-depth explanations about these stages and what to look for in others or yourself.

1. Physical Relapse

How To Stop Drinking Alcohol Today

This stage includes an actual decision to use alcohol again. When an alcoholic hits this stage, some might continue using it for months but others will realize what they did and begin to refocus on their recovery.

A common strategy is replacing your current alcoholism with some positive activities. There are several things you can do to help fill what may feel like a hole in your life.

Here are some activities that could help prevent a relapse:

- Volunteering

When you help others, it will just reinforce your decision that you want to help yourself. There won't ever be a wrong time to encourage others or yourself.

- Sports

Getting involved in sports will allow you to commit to yourself positively while getting the benefits of socializing and exercising.

- Reading

This is a great way to expand your mind while keeping your brain occupied and away from tempting, harmful thoughts.

- Socializing

It is very important to socialize. It is best if you socialize with the correct people. When you socialize with family and friends that support you, it keeps you heading in the right direction during your recovery.

- Entertainment

Going to the movies or a show are great distractions to keep your focus away from anything that you might be going through.

- Crafts

Creating jewelry, sewing, tie-dying shirts, DIY projects, etc. can be a great way to let you find accomplishment and joy through creative challenges.

How To Stop Drinking Alcohol Today

- Art

Sculpting, writing, painting, music, etc. are ways to challenge your brain to become creative. These activities are great coping mechanisms because they help you to express yourself.

- Games

Video, card, and board games are great distractions for anyone in recovery. These are all safe activities to keep you away from alcohol.

- Exercise

Yoga, walking, weights and running are all ways to release endorphins that let you feel alive in natural and healthy ways.

- Tasks

Cleaning, ironing, sweeping, washing the dishes, and cooking are all activities that give you a sense of empowerment and can create an environment that helps support your sobriety.

2. Mental Relapse

At this stage, your mind is battling between trying to decide whether or not to drink. Part of an alcoholic wants to drink but another part doesn't want them to.

Some signs of a mental relapse might include planning a relapse, thinking about relapse, spending time with other alcoholics, lying, glamorizing alcoholism, and reminiscing about the places and people you used to hang around with.

Most of the time, recovering alcoholics are the only people who can pinpoint these symptoms as internal battles. Other people won't be able to pick up on these symptoms.

If you realize that a mental relapse is beginning, there are some techniques an alcoholic could use to get control of their thoughts and make the right choice of not drinking. Here are four techniques you can try that will prevent a mental relapse:

- Call somebody

It could be a family member, friend, or your sponsor. Talking through your urges with somebody else could help you figure out why you want to drink and they can tell you why you shouldn't. Talking with another person will make the reasons for relapse less intimidating. It will make all the reasons why you want to drink again seem less logical. Talking with others will bring you clarity as to why drinking isn't going to solve any of your problems but will just create more.

- Wait 30 minutes

Before you act impulsively, wait at least 30 minutes and then reevaluate your reasons and urges. Waiting on time to pass could help clear your mind.

- What could happen if you drank

Usually, it won't stop with one drink and you might find yourself at the same low you hit before if it isn't a deeper one. Think about your actions and consequences as this could curb your desire to drink.

- Don't worry about each day. Worry about today

People who have been sober for a very long time still take their sobriety day by day. If you think about it in years or even forever, this gets too intimidating and could result in being overwhelmed and needing to drink.

Rather than thinking in terms of forever, focus on trying to make it through each day without drinking. Then do this again the next day, and then repeat it the following day. Pretty soon, the days are going to add up.

3. Emotional Relapse

At this stage, you aren't actively thinking about drinking. Your actions or behaviors might be setting you up to go down the road of relapse instead.

Emotional relapse might be detected by symptoms like bad eating or sleeping habits, not attending meetings, isolation, mood swings, defensiveness, anger, intolerance, and anxiety.

During this stage of relapse, it will be aligned with post-acute withdrawal syndrome where an alcoholic will experience psychological and emotional withdrawals instead of physical ones.

Physical withdrawals will last just a few weeks to about two years after you stop drinking. Episodes of physical withdrawals might last a couple of days and might include the above symptoms.

Dealing With A Relapse Or Slip

The easiest way to keep from relapsing or slipping up is to act immediately. It isn't anything that you can do by yourself. How serious the slip is shouldn't be downplayed by anyone including you. It doesn't matter how minor or serious the slip might be; this is a sign that something is terribly wrong and there are problems that have to be worked out so it doesn't happen again.

It is never enough just to commit to quitting. You have to find the reasons behind this slip and figure out what triggered it. If you don't do some serious soul-searching, you won't be able to keep from slipping if the same problem arises again.

If you do have a relapse or slip, there is something you have to immediately do: Pick yourself up and continue with the program.

Don't act like nothing happened. You need to continue to move forward. There are some steps you need to do immediately to make sure the relapse stops:

- Stay in perspective – this isn't the end of the world

How To Stop Drinking Alcohol Today

- Get yourself out of the situation

- Get in touch with your sponsor

- Don't be alone; call your support group to be with you

- Find a meeting. Go to as many meeting as you possibly can. The things you hear at the meeting could save your life.

- Read some articles about addiction and recovery

- Don't wallow in guilt or shame

- Clean yourself up. You are going to feel better.

- Eat something healthy. Never mistake hunger pangs for alcohol cravings.

Basically, you shouldn't feel guilty about slipping. The only thing that matters is that you need to take it seriously and know that it's a mistake that you need to learn from.

But if you have relapsed and have committed to recovery again, there are some things you need to remember:

- Don't feel guilty, you just have to double up your efforts to reach and keep your sobriety.

- Because you are committing again, it means that you realize how deep your addiction is.

- Don't be ashamed of your mistakes, face them head on and find out what you have to do to not make them again.

- You don't have to feel as if you have lost completely and have gone back to day one. Everything you do in life will show you that your recovery keeps going forward. Anyone who has stayed sober for more than one day might experience sobriety in profound ways.

This will be different for somebody who has been sober for over a year. Use these feelings to keep moving forward.

In the long run, you need to rededicate yourself to the recovery program. Talk about any concerns or problems you might be having with your counselor or therapist. They know how to deal with relapses and can help you through this one.

If you have gone through an actual rehab program but relapsed, talk with your support system and sponsor to see if they think you should go back to rehab. A relapse is just one bump in the long road to sobriety. Remind yourself that the only failure is to stop believing in yourself. Don't ever give up.

Conclusion

Thank you for making it through to the end of *How to Stop Drinking Alcohol Today*. Let's hope it was informative and able to provide you with all of the tools you need to stop drinking for good.

Giving up alcohol is tough, but it is well worth the effort. With the right mindset, a sound support system and the right tools, you will be able to quit drinking for good. You've made a fantastic first step in reading this book. The next thing you need to do is to create your goals and find some other people who can support you. Look to find a local AA meeting and get a sponsor.

Sobriety is a long road that never really ends, but it does get easier. There will be times where you will want to give up, but lean on your sponsor, family, friends, and other tools you have. You will get through this, I'm sure of it.

How To Stop Drinking Alcohol Today

Finally, if you found this book useful in any way, a review on Amazon is always appreciated!

Connect with us on our Facebook page www.facebook.com/bluesourceandfriends and stay tuned to our latest book promotions and free giveaways.

CPSIA information can be obtained
at www.ICGtesting.com
Printed in the USA
BVHW032055011019
559918BV00001B/77/P

9 781690 495512